W9-AYX-766

Picture Credits:
AKG: 4, 22 (bottom), 23, 24, 34, 41 (both), 48, 51; Bettmann; Bridgeman Art Library: 18-19 (top), 26-27 (top), 26 (bottom), 30-31 (top); Christie's Colour Library: Explorer; Gamma; Hulton Deutsch Collection; Image Select; Mary Evans; Novosti; International Red Cross and Red Crescent Movement (Geneva); Robert Harding; Scala; Society for Cultural Relations; Tretyakof Gallery; Zefa.

The author wishes to express his thanks to the librarian and staff of Swaffham and Watton branches of Norfolk County Library, and to Harold Tyler, for their invaluable help.

Published in Great Britain in 1992
by Exley Publications Ltd,
16 Chalk Hill, Watford,
Herts WD1 4BN, United Kingdom.

Copyright © Exley Publications, 1992
Copyright © Michael Pollard, 1992

**A copy of the CIP data is available from
the British Library on request**

ISBN 1-85015-303-5

Series editor: Helen Exley
Editor: Samantha Armstrong
Picture editor: Alex Goldberg of Image Select
Music and Education advisor: Jill Simms
Typeset by Brush Off Studios,
St Albans, Herts AL3 4PH.
Printed in Spain by Gráficas Reunidas, S.A.

Peter Ilyich
TCHAIKOVSKY

Michael Pollard

ꕕEXLEY

Secret admirer

In December 1876 a letter from an unknown woman arrived at the Moscow home of the composer Peter Ilyich Tchaikovsky.

It was a short letter, partly of thanks, partly fan mail. Through a friend and former pupil, Tchaikovsky had been commissioned by this anonymous woman to make arrangements for violin and piano of some of his pieces so that she could play them at home. It was work that he enjoyed doing. It could be done quickly – and the fee offered was generous. He had finished the arrangements in only a few days. The letter was the response. "Your music makes life pleasanter and easier to live," his mysterious admirer wrote.

It was the start of a strange friendship that was to last for fourteen years – almost to the end of Tchaikovsky's life. It was remarkable in many ways. The two – composer and admirer – met only a few times, and then by accident. They never spoke to each other. Yet they exchanged hundreds of letters, revealing and discussing their innermost thoughts. Although both sometimes wrote with deep feeling, confessing their love for each other, their relationship never developed into a love affair.

In fact Tchaikovsky was homosexual, and his admirer, who had had twelve children, took a fairly poor view of physical love. She became his patron, paying him an annual income which relieved him from financial worries during the most creative period of his life. But three years before his death she broke off the friendship as suddenly as she had begun it, with an excuse that turned out to be a lie.

Tchaikovsky's admirer was a widow in her midforties, Madame Nadia von Meck. Tchaikovsky was thirty-six. Nadia von Meck was extremely rich. She and her late husband had built up a vastly profitable railroad construction business. When he died suddenly, she inherited two companies, together with large estates, forests, farms and valuable

Opposite: Peter Ilyich Tchaikovsky was a haunted man, tortured by self-doubt and fear of failure. Here, in his fifties, he looks older – despite being able to look back on a life of musical achievement which brought lasting pleasure to many people.

Below: Nadia von Meck, whose relationship with the composer brought him happiness, great distress and confusion.

5

investments. Her marriage had not been a particularly happy one, but its end left her with time on her hands. She filled this by taking an interest in the musical life of Moscow.

Nadia von Meck was an accomplished amateur pianist, and she took on to her domestic staff a young violinist, Josef Kotek, with whom to play duets. It was through Kotek, his former pupil, that Tchaikovsky had received the first commission from her, and that the wealthy widow had heard of the composer's shortage of money.

It was as a result of this introduction that Tchaikovsky gained the financial security that enabled him to fill the remainder of his life with the creation of his finest work; work for which he would be remembered as one of the world's leading composers.

Lost music

Tchaikovsky's international reputation rests on a fairly small part of his music. Much of his work has never been performed outside his native country. Of the ten operas that he wrote, only two are known outside Russia and neither is performed very often. Some of his music has been lost altogether. The quality of his most famous work, ballet music such as *Swan Lake* and *The Sleeping Beauty*, was not recognized until after his death because the ballets were produced so badly in his lifetime.

Music critics have often dismissed Tchaikovsky as a lightweight composer. This may be because his gift for easily-remembered melodies, such as the opening theme of his first piano concerto, makes his music easy for non-musicians to enjoy. But his work has also attracted the admiration of leading orchestral conductors and soloists from the nineteenth century up to the present day.

Doubt

Both personally and professionally, Tchaikovsky's was a strange life, and for the most part an unhappy one. He longed for acceptance by the musical world, both in Russia and abroad. But – especially in his early days – he defied the conventions of what the musical world expected. Even after his reputation was established, his music was often savagely criticized. He strove for perfection – but he was also often tempted to dash off quick pieces against the clock simply to make some money. In his personal life, he looked back with longing to the happy years of his childhood, and sideways to the similar family atmosphere of his sister Sasha and her children. Yet he was prevented by his homosexual nature – and by society's attitude to it – from ever creating even a similar setting for his own life. His attempt at marriage brought him to the verge of madness and suicide. And even near the end of his life, when he was admired internationally, he was tortured by doubt about his own worth, both as a composer and as a person.

A provincial life

Peter Ilyich Tchaikovsky was born on May 7, 1840 in Votinsk, an iron-mining town to the east of Moscow, Russia. His father was a government inspector at the mines. Peter's mother was his father's second wife, the first having died.

The Tchaikovskys had a comfortable lifestyle. Peter's father, Ilya, was a rather dull man who devoted his attention to providing for his family, but had little contact with his children. Peter had a brother, Nicholas, two years older than himself and a sister, Sasha, two years younger. In 1844 another brother, Hippolyte, was born. Peter's mother, Alexandra, was fluent in French and German and had some amateur musical ability. The family was sufficiently wealthy to afford a number of servants and a governess for the children.

In 1848, Peter's father decided to take a job in Moscow, then Russia's second city.

The move was a disaster. The job Ilya had been hoping for had been taken when they arrived, and the city was in the grip of a cholera epidemic. Cholera, spreading like wildfire and almost inevitably fatal, was the scourge of nineteenth

"You are needed by us .... by Russia," claimed Tchaikovsky's teacher and friend, Nikolay Rubinstein. Tchaikovsky was very proud to be Russian and his music was influenced by its traditions and its people. For many Russians, life was one of endless hard work for few rewards, like these serfs hauling a boat on the great trading river, the Volga.

century Europe. It spread in waves from the Far East, and hit Russia on its way westwards. Disappointed over his hoped-for job and terrified by the epidemic, Peter's father took the family to the Russian capital, St. Petersburg. Then, when he found work as a mine manager in a remote part of Russia near the Siberian border, they moved on again. But it was decided that Peter should be educated in St. Petersburg, and he was sent to stay with friends. By this time – he was now ten – the comfortable and loving environment in which he had spent his first eight years had been thoroughly disturbed. He was to spend much of his adult life depressed and longing for the care and security of his early childhood. As he grew older his memories seemed even more magic and desirable.

Backward Russia

So far, there had not been the slightest hint that Tchaikovsky's future lay with music. The school he was sent to in St. Petersburg trained its pupils for the government service. This was not a surprising

choice on the part of his parents. His father was a government inspector. The government service offered a safe, fairly well-paid career with scope for promotion and for travel to different parts of greater Russia.

The Russia in which Tchaikovsky was born was vast, thinly populated and, compared with western Europe, backward. The Industrial Revolution, which was changing the face of Europe, had not yet reached the East. Russia's people were mostly peasants, tied to their work on the land. There was no Russian parliament. The country was ruled by the Tsar, who had absolute power over his people. With his advisers – who knew better than to advise anything that they knew he would not agree with – he made the law. Vast numbers of government servants collected taxes and inspected all the activities of the people to make sure that no one was getting away without paying. These inspectors, forever prying and reporting, stood in the way of real progress. But the government service provided careers for people with some education, and this was the background from which the Tchaikovsky family came.

When Tchaikovsky was born, Russia was not a progressive country. While Western Europe had developed steam power to make building more efficient, Russia was still using manpower. Most Russians were tied to their work on the land and had little education. But to train for the government was a good career so Tchaikovsky was sent to school in St. Petersburg to become a clerk.

Dreadful news

Tchaikovsky, aged fourteen, was settling into the senior school at St. Petersburg when he received dreadful news. His mother had suddenly died of cholera. At school, he had been homesick but he had always been able to comfort himself with his store of memories of the happy family at home, of which his mother was at the heart. Now, there would be no more memories to add to the store.

He was heartbroken. The family broke up. Tchaikovsky's brother Hippolyte was sent to a boarding school for naval cadets and his beloved sister Sasha to a girls' boarding school. His twin brothers Anatol and Modest, who were only four, were to be looked after by their uncle and aunt.

It was around this time that Tchaikovsky began to take more of an interest in music. Perhaps it was a way of trying to forget his unhappiness. He took

singing and piano lessons. However, when the question came up as to whether he should make his career in music, Tchaikovsky's teacher, Rudolf Kundinger, in a letter to Tchaikovsky's father which was to cause Kundinger embarrassment later in life, advised against it. He saw no sign of genius in the sixteen-year-old Tchaikovsky and could not recommend him for a musical career.

But many people get pleasure out of music without necessarily wanting to make a career of it. Tchaikovsky continued to enjoy playing, experimenting with composition, and studying opera. As for his career plans, he continued as an undistinguished student until the school turned him into what it was designed to – a junior clerk. In 1859, Tchaikovsky started work in the Ministry of Justice in St. Petersburg. So, aged nineteen, with his salary in his pocket, he enjoyed the opportunities St. Petersburg had to offer: plays, opera, ballet and social evenings with musical friends.

Right: The piano Tchaikovsky played as a boy, now in the Tchaikovsky Museum at Votinsk. When he was very young, he began to take an interest in music, but, at first, he was discouraged by his governess, Fanny Durbach. She could see that music had a disturbing effect on him. On one occasion, she found him in bed clapping his hand to his head and crying, "Oh, this music, this music! Take it away! It's in here and it won't let me sleep!"

The musical desert

Rudolf Kundinger's coolness about the idea of music as a career for his pupil was not only the result of his low opinion of Tchaikovsky's ability. The fact was that, in Russia, music did not offer much of a career. The great upsurge of musical creativity that had flooded through western Europe and produced composers like Bach, Mozart, Haydn and Beethoven had not reached Russia. Music flourished in western Europe because of the support, or patronage, of royalty and noble families who maintained composers and musicians to provide them with all kinds of musical fare, ranging from light pieces to accompany their meals to full-scale operas to entertain their guests. Music did not receive the same kind of support at the court of Tsar Nicholas II or among his nobles.

As an art, music had low status and there was hardly any musical education. Most successful Russian composers wrote music in their spare time, earning their living from some other profession, rather than being employed by a patron. Alexander Borodin, for example, was a professor of chemistry. Modest Mussorgsky and Nikolay Rimsky-Korsakov had military careers.

Change

But a change took place about the time that Tchaikovsky started work at the Ministry of Justice. The result was that he became the first important Russian composer to have received his musical education in his own country – and one of the first to make music his full-time profession. Tchaikovsky took advantage of this opportunity to give his country music a particularly Russian feel. Tsar Alexander II had a German-born aunt, the Grand Duchess Elena Pavlovna, who had visited western Europe with a young pianist and composer, Anton Rubinstein. They returned fired with enthusiasm to put Russia on the musical map. In 1859 the Grand Duchess persuaded her nephew, the Tsar, to back her. In September that year she set up, in her home at the Mikhailovsky Palace in St. Petersburg with

Tsar Alexander II's aunt, the Grand Duchess Elena Pavlovna, was the driving-force behind the birth of a truly Russian musical culture. With the pianist and composer, Anton Rubinstein, she formed the Russian Musical Society and founded the St. Petersburg Conservatoire. From then on, Russian composers began to take pride in their own distinctive style, and stopped looking over their shoulders at what was happening in the musical capitals of western Europe.

Anton Rubinstein in charge, the Russian Musical Society. Its aim was to make music more important in Russian life.

Within two years the Russian Musical Society had outgrown its quarters at the palace. With the Tsar's support, Elena Pavlovna opened the St. Petersburg Conservatoire, or music college, in a larger building on the bank of the River Neva. By that time, something had happened in Tchaikovsky's life which was to draw him and the new mood of Russian music together.

The sounds of Europe

In July 1861, Tchaikovsky took time off work at the Ministry and set out on a tour of Europe with a friend of his father's. They took in Germany, Belgium, Holland and France – seeing the new technology of the Industrial Revolution and hearing the music. But Tchaikovsky spent recklessly and returned to St. Petersburg three months later alone and in debt. His dream of making music into a career, however, had been revived. He was excited by his experience of countries where music was taken seriously.

Did he have enough talent? Did Russia offer the kind of opportunities he had observed on his travels? Or was his dream to remain just that?

Sasha's marriage

Shortly after Tchaikovsky had started work at the Ministry of Justice, his sister Sasha married. He got on well with all his brothers and sisters, but his relationship with Sasha had been special. In their teenage years they had been inseparable companions. They had written regularly and at great length to each other when they were apart. Now, with Sasha's marriage, it seemed to the sensitive Tchaikovsky that yet another link with his childhood was being broken, especially since her married home was to be at Kamenka in the Ukraine, a long way from St. Petersburg.

Kamenka was a large country house on a vast

Russians had a deeply-felt instinct for family life in the style pictured here. After the upheaval of moving to St. Petersburg, having to stay at boarding school and the death of his mother, Tchaikovsky always tried to recapture the essence of his early childhood. He longed to recreate the happy, loving and secure atmosphere of the family.

estate owned by the aristocratic family into which Sasha had married, the Davidovs. In fact, Kamenka was to provide him with a refuge for most of his life, and Sasha's children were to be a substitute for the children he never had. There was a well-stocked library, rooms in which Tchaikovsky could study or compose, and delightful countryside in which to walk. He was to spend much of his free time at Kamenka, and a lot of his music was written there. And, despite his fears when Sasha married, his relationship with her remained close. At the time, however, Sasha's marriage seemed like another blow of fate, taking away the person he held most dear.

One of the major influences on Tchaikovsky's personality was his regret that, as a homosexual, he would never have the family life he loved. When his sister, Sasha, married into the Davidov family he found refuge in their country estate, Kamenka, pictured below, in the Ukraine. He spent many happy months there.

Dedicated to music

There was no family money to support Tchaikovsky in his musical ambitions. His father was living on a small government pension, with two now teenage sons, Modest and Anatol, to bring up. Tchaikovsky could not risk – at least until he had some idea of what his chances were of making a career out of music – giving up his dull but safe and reasonably well-paid job at the Ministry of Justice. So he kept on working there, but also enrolled at the new Conservatoire to study harmony and composition in his spare time. But by the spring of 1863, aged twenty-three, he was confident enough to resign from the Ministry and become a full-time student. He planned to pay for his studies by giving private music lessons.

Student

The decision enabled Tchaikovsky for the first time to live a complete life of music. He studied all day. In the evenings he would play piano duets with a new friend from the Conservatoire, Hermann Laroche, or join in musical evenings with other students. It soon became clear that Tchaikovsky was an outstanding and very hard-working student. Anton Rubinstein, now the director of the Conservatoire as well as Tchaikovsky's tutor in composition, told a story of an occasion when he set his class to write some variations on a theme. He expected about twelve variations – but Tchaikovsky handed in over two hundred.

At the Conservatoire, Tchaikovsky seems to have managed to keep his moods of black depression at bay – until almost the last moment. It was the rule that each student should compose a graduation piece to be performed by the Conservatoire orchestra. Tchaikovsky was set to write a choral setting for Schiller's poem *Ode to Joy*, the same poem that provides the theme of the last movement of Beethoven's Ninth Symphony. It must have been quite a challenge for a twenty-five-year-old student to produce a piece that would inevitably be compared with Beethoven's masterly setting of forty

Tchaikovsky in 1863, when, at twenty-three, he resigned from his government job and began full-time study at the St. Petersburg Conservatoire. This was a courageous step, for he had to support himself while studying. But as he wrote to his sister, Sasha, "I only want to do the work for which I have a vocation. Whether I become a famous composer or a struggling teacher, it's all the same."

years earlier. However the second half of the graduation ceremony was a session at which the student was questioned by a panel of distinguished musicians. Always sensitive to criticism, and always doubtful of his own worth, Tchaikovsky could not face this. He failed to turn up. Rubinstein was furious – he threatened not to award Tchaikovsky his diploma. But in the end he relented, and Tchaikovsky graduated in 1865 from the St. Petersburg Conservatoire with a silver medal.

Move to Moscow

The Grand Duchess Elena Pavlovna, in founding the Russian Musical Society, had created a great thirst for music in Russia. The St. Petersburg branch had been followed by another in Moscow which was directed by Nicolas Rubinstein, the brother of Anton. By 1865 this had grown into the Moscow Conservatoire, a music college, and after Tchaikovsky graduated he took a post as tutor in harmony there. The pay was poor, but it was just about enough to live on. In January 1866, Tchaikovsky arrived in Moscow to start his new job.

The move meant that he had to make a new social life for himself in a strange city. Although Rubinstein eased Tchaikovsky's way into Moscow life by taking him into his own house and introducing him to his friends, Tchaikovsky was homesick. "Moscow is a strange place," he wrote to Sasha, "and it will be long before I can contemplate without horror the thought of remaining here for years – perhaps for ever." To occupy his homesick mind, and to show that he was musically "independent" and not bound to the musical views of the Rubinsteins, he began work almost at once on his First Symphony in G Minor.

The new age in Russian musical life opened by the Grand Duchess was only a few years old, but already a rift had begun to appear. The St. Petersburg and Moscow Conservatoires, directed by the Rubinstein brothers, wanted to identify Russia with the western European musical tradition. But many of their students – Tchaikovsky among them – did

Starting out on his new life as a musician, Tchaikovsky gave private music lessons to pay for his studies at the Conservatoire. His lifestyle had to be tempered – living in a small plain room, less drinking with Nicolas Rubinstein and fewer visits to plays and concerts. Despite this simple way of life, Tchaikovsky had never been happier.

Moscow, where Tchaikovsky arrived in January 1866 to teach at the new Conservatoire. To his surprise, his classes were successful and the nervousness that he had anticipated vanished quickly. He was soon involved in the lively academic and social life of Russia's second city.

not want to be mere copiers. They aimed to be originators. They wanted to create a distinctively national style, incorporating the life and enthusiasm of Russian folk music. This did not only mean using folk tunes in their work – though Tchaikovsky sometimes did this – but also choosing themes in the *style* of Russian folk music, with its distinctive rhythms and harmonies.

Tchaikovsky had spent the first eight years of his life deep inside Russia. With his acute ear for melody and rhythm, he would have absorbed this folk influence from an early age. When he came to write music, the *technique* of composition was something he learned at the Conservatoire but he applied it to this *understanding* of the old, traditional music-making of the people. Throughout his life, both in Russia and abroad, he listened for and often noted down tunes sung by people in the streets or the fields.

Some of Tchaikovsky's student work had reflected all this, and one of his pieces, an Overture in C minor, was condemned by both Rubinstein brothers. They refused to let it be played by the Conservatoire orchestras. It would not, in fact, be performed until 1931, thirty-eight years after Tchaikovsky's death.

First Symphony

So Tchaikovsky was in a defiant mood when, in March 1866, he started to work on his First Symphony. Almost at once he was struck down by a fit of depression deeper than any he had experienced before. He could not sleep. He suffered from migraines and what he called "apopleptic strokes", possibly a mild form of epilepsy. Composition went "sluggishly", and he became obsessed with the idea that he would die before his symphony was finished. He was kept going in the spring months by the thought of his planned visit with Sasha and her family at Kamenka.

But, as it turned out, the roads were so bad that the journey was impossible.

Instead he arranged to spend the summer with Sasha's mother-in-law and her daughters, Vera and Elizabeta, who did not live so far away. At first, Tchaikovsky felt calm and rested in the quiet beauty of the country. But as soon as he started working on his symphony again, his health became worse. Nightmares, hallucinations and numbness in his arms and legs added to his troubles. By August, a doctor told Tchaikovsky's family that he was "one step away from insanity" and ordered him to take a complete rest from both playing and composition.

Tchaikovsky's recovery was swift, but he had learned a frightening lesson. He swore that he would never again compose at such a furious pace, and he never did. But by September he was in St. Petersburg showing the first draft of the symphony to his old teacher Anton Rubinstein. He hoped for

"One thing troubles me: there is no one in Moscow with whom I can enter into really intimate, familiar and homely relations. I often think how happy I should be if you, or someone like you, lived here. I have a great longing for the sound of children's voices, and for a share in all the trifling interests of a home – in a word, for family life."
Tchaikovsky, writing to his sister, Sasha, February 1870.

"As regards the Russian element in my works, I may tell you that not infrequently I begin a composition with the intention of introducing some folk-melody into it. Sometimes it comes of its own accord, unintentionally.... As to this national element in my work, its affinity with the folksongs in some of my melodies and harmonies proceeds from my having spent my childhood in the country and having, from my earliest years, been impregnated with the characteristic beauty of our Russian folk-music.... I am Russian in the fullest sense of the word."
Tchaikovsky, writing to Nadia von Meck, March 1878.

17

encouragement, but he was disappointed. Rubinstein said that the symphony was not fit to perform. He reworked parts of it, and the two middle movements were played that winter in Moscow and St. Petersburg. But the applause was lukewarm. It was not until February 1868 that the complete symphony was performed and, according to Tchaikovsky himself, "scored a great success". Yet it was not heard again for another fifteen years, and then in a revised form. Tchaikovsky's first major work, written at such risk to his mental health, had turned out to be a relative failure.

Tchaikovsky had tried to express in his First Symphony one of the central themes of his life – his love of the Russian countryside. He gave the symphony the title *Winter Daydreams*. The first movement was headed "Daydreams on the wintry road" and the second "Sullen land, foggy land". It was important to him to make such emotional and pictorial links in his music. "I shouldn't like," he

Above: Russian peasants return from work in the fields at sunset. This was the kind of winter landscape that inspired Tchaikovsky's First Symphony. The solemn Russian countryside was to be a recurring theme in Tchaikovsky's work.
Opposite: A fair. Apart from trading, fairs were occasions for singing and dancing to traditional folk music – music to which Tchaikovsky turned for inspiration. However, Tchaikovsky also used French and German influences in his compositions.

once wrote, "a symphonic production expressing nothing and consisting of an empty play of chords, rhythms and modulations to come from my pen."

But it was this very personal touch in his music that upset his teachers and critics. They preferred clever demonstrations of composing technique – "an empty play of chords, rhythms and modulations" – to the emotional involvement that Tchaikovsky's music offered. This is, even today, an attitude that some critics take to his work.

Longing for a family

It was about this time, in the early years of his career, that Tchaikovsky came face to face with his own internal emotional turmoil. He had recognized by now – as hints in his letters make clear – that he was homosexual by nature. In nineteenth-century Russia, as in most countries, homosexuality was not uncommon, but it was something that was not talked about. A career in music depended on the support of "polite society", and a successful composer, like any other professional person, was expected to have a settled marriage and family life. But Tchaikovsky's problem was not only what other people expected. He himself longed for the kind of family life he could remember from his early childhood and that he saw at Sasha's home. The key to that kind of life was a happy marriage.

He was made keenly aware of this on his visit to the Baltic with Sasha's in-laws, the Davidov family, in the summer of 1867. There, an attractive Davidov daughter, Vera, fell in love with him. To his discomfort, she made no secret of her feelings. Tchaikovsky hoped, as he confided to Sasha, that "daily contact with my far from poetic qualities such as slovenliness, irritability, cowardice, triviality, self-esteem, secretiveness, and so on" would put her off. But he undid these stern hopes by dedicating to Vera Davidova three piano pieces which he wrote that summer. (They included *Song without words,* one of his best-known piano compositions.) Tchaikovsky and Vera had also, during that time, talked of "future farmhouses of our own, where we might quietly live out our days." Vera Davidova naturally took these as encouraging signs of Tchaikovsky's interest in her. But by the next year Tchaikovsky was urgently seeking his sister's advice on how he could avoid being trapped into marriage. He was, he said, "too lazy" to take on the responsibilities of marriage and a family, fond though he was of Vera. "I feel that I would conceive a hatred for her if the question of fulfilling our relationship in marriage should become serious." But Vera had evidently put marriage into Tchaikovsky's mind, for within a few weeks he had fallen genuinely in love.

Tchaikovsky's sister, Sasha, and her husband, Lev Davidov, about the time of their marriage in 1860. Sasha made what was known in those days as a "good marriage". The Davidovs had large estates, like Kamenka, which they managed to hold on to despite Lev's father having been involved in a plot against Tsar Nicholas I.

In love

Désirée Artôt was a thirty-two-year-old Belgian soprano with an international reputation. She came to Moscow in 1868 with a touring Italian opera company. Tchaikovsky's admiration of her singing developed rapidly into something more – he wrote pieces and arrangements for her, and sent long letters to his family confessing his love for her. His friends pointed out that she was already famous, and four years his senior. If he married her, he would become "Artôt's husband", living in her shadow. Tchaikovsky, now twenty-nine, announced their engagement to his father and asked his advice. Whose career should come first – Désirée's, already established, or his own, at its very beginning? "I shall be deprived of the chance of going forward along my own road if I follow her blindly ... but all the forces in my heart bind me to her, and at the present moment it seems to me impossible to live my whole life without her."

As it turned out, the problem solved itself – or rather, was solved by Désirée. In her absence in Warsaw, Tchaikovsky busied himself with rehearsals for his first opera, *The Voyevoda*. Like his First Symphony, this had been a struggle to complete, and it was now going into production with an orchestra that was too small, scenery adapted from other operas, and singers who were not up to the standard he demanded. As the opening night approached, tension both on and off the stage grew to fever pitch. Then, in the middle of rehearsals, Nicolas Rubinstein came on to the stage with a telegram. Désirée Artôt, in Warsaw, had married a Spanish singer.

Rubinstein made no effort to hide his relief. Tchaikovsky, according to reports, went white and walked out. But it seems that it was his pride rather than his heart that was hurt. Within a few days he was working harder than ever on *The Voyevoda*, shrugging off whatever pain he felt. What caused him more anguish was that his opera was a failure. It was savaged by the critics, who said it lacked Russian temperament and was too heavily influenced by German and Italian music. It was taken

Above: Désirée Artôt, with whom Tchaikovsky first fell in love.
Below: Tchaikovsky's first teacher, Anton Rubinstein.

off after five performances in spite of an enthusiastic first night audience. He destroyed most of the score, and only a few fragments exist today.

Down to work

The summer of 1869 found Tchaikovsky at a low ebb. His courtship of Désirée Artôt had ended in humiliation. However relieved he might have felt that he no longer had to face a choice between his future wife's career and his own, he must have been acutely aware of the sniggers of the Moscow gossips. His first two large works, the Symphony in G Minor and *The Voyevoda*, had been failures. That summer he retreated to the place where he felt most secure and untroubled – Kamenka.

It was a turning-point in Tchaikovsky's life. There followed one of his most creative periods, which saw the composition of many of the works by which he is remembered today. On his return from Kamenka, his sister's country home, he started writing the fantasy overture to *Romeo and Juliet*. The next few years saw the composition of the Second Symphony in C Minor, music for *The Snow Maiden* and Shakespeare's *The Tempest*, three String Quartets, the Third Symphony in D Major, and the *Swan Lake* ballet music.

Other works in this period ranged from piano arrangements of fifty Russian folk songs to three operas. Tchaikovsky broke away finally from the restrictions imposed by the Rubinsteins and his other teachers, and began to compose in his own distinctive way – often to their disapproval. He was not afraid to use great sweeping melodies, given added life by his use of the instruments of the orchestra, to create music aimed at the emotions rather than the intellect.

This approach to music brought both pain and rewards. The critics were mostly reticent in their praise of Tchaikovsky's work. Some condemned it outright. To many of his teachers, he was breaking the rules by writing in such a directly emotional way.

But audiences received his music quite differently. They responded with enthusiasm, and the

A scene from Shakespeare's "Romeo and Juliet", for which Tchaikovsky wrote his Fantasy Overture in 1869. It was a failure on its first performance in Moscow in the spring of 1870, but it has since become one of Tchaikovsky's best-loved works, with its open and uninhibited commitment to emotion.

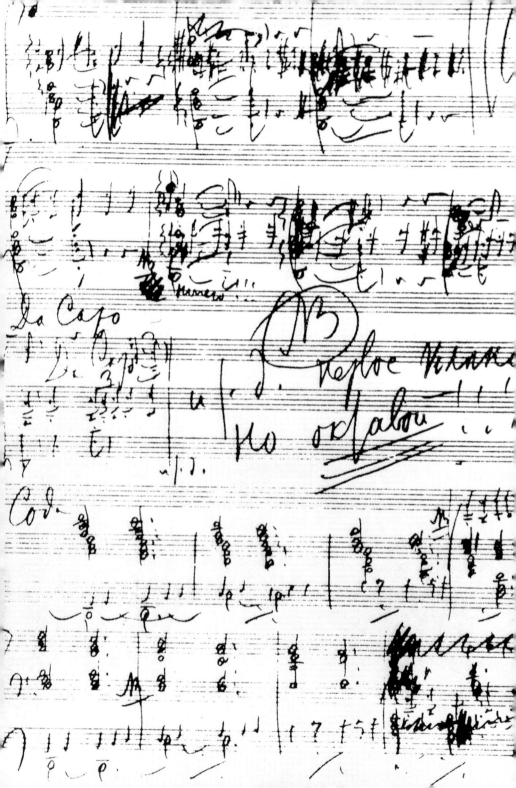

accessibility of his work brought into the concert halls a new kind of audience – music-lovers who were not academically trained but who were there simply to enjoy the musical effects that Tchaikovsky could produce. His reputation in western Europe began to grow. Then, late in 1875, it made a leap across the Atlantic.

Opposite: A page from Tchaikovsky's original score for his Sixth Symphony. All his working life, Tchaikovsky saw himself as a professional composer and would work constantly – rather than wait for inspiration. Something of the agony of composition is reflected here.

The "worthless" concerto

Tchaikovsky had turned, for his next work, to the shorter concerto form – a work, usually in three movements, in which the main themes are carried by a solo instrument with the orchestra providing the setting. He began writing his Piano Concerto No. 1 in 1874, and for once composition went smoothly. Within two months he had finished it, and decided to play it to Nicolas Rubinstein in the hope that Rubinstein would give it its first performance. The two met at the Moscow Conservatoire on Christmas Eve, 1874. Tchaikovsky himself takes up the story, in a letter written three years later: "I played the first movement. Never a word, never a single remark. Do you know the awkward and ridiculous sensation of putting before a friend a meal which you have cooked yourself, which he eats – and holds his tongue? Oh for a single word, for friendly abuse, for *anything* to break the silence! For God's sake say *something!* But Rubinstein never opened his lips…. I gathered patience and played the concerto straight through to the end. Still silence.

"'Well?' I asked, and rose from the piano. Then a torrent broke from Rubinstein's lips…. My concerto was worthless, absolutely unplayable…. Only one or two pages were worth anything. All the rest had better be destroyed or entirely rewritten….

"I left the room without a word and went upstairs. I could not have spoken for anger and agitation. Presently Rubinstein came to me and, seeing how upset I was, called me into another room. There he repeated that my concerto was impossible, pointed out many places where it needed to be completely revised, and said if I would suit the

Below: Thirty-three-year-old Tchaikovsky in 1873, the year in which his Second Symphony was performed. "It is a long time," wrote one critic, "since I have encountered a work of art with … such well motivated and artistically worked-out contrasts." It was his first unqualified success.

25

Left: The Russian Orthodox Church attached great importance to ritual, and this fondness for the ceremonial communicated itself to the Russian people. In turn, it was reflected in the music of Russian composers, including Tchaikovsky. The wedding procession here is reminiscent of the wedding music in Tchaikovsky's "Undine" which also appears in the slow movement of his Second Symphony. The symphony is known as the "Little Russian" because it includes Ukrainian folk songs.

concerto to his requirements he would bring it out at his concert. 'I shall not alter a single note,' I replied. 'I shall publish the work precisely as it stands.'"

A different opinion

He was as good as his word, and went ahead with the full scoring of the concerto ready for its orchestral performance. But it may have been Rubinstein's scorn that led Tchaikovsky to allow its first performance – a triumphant one, as it turned out – to be given in Boston, United States. The soloist was Hans von Bülow, possibly the most famous pianist and conductor of his day, who was at that time on a world tour. Bülow's opinion of Tchaikovsky's concerto was the absolute opposite of Rubinstein's. "The ideas," he wrote, "are so lofty, strong and original.... The form is so perfect, mature, and full of style.... I should grow weary if I attempted

Opposite below: A religious procession, with banners and holy relics being carried to the church. Harshly treated as the Russian people were by rulers and employers, religion, its music and grandeur, was one of their few consolations. It was a part of Russian life which nationalistic composers like "The Five" – a group of five Russian composers – and Tchaikovsky would use in their music.

27

The Moscow Conservatoire, where Tchaikovsky taught from its opening in 1866 until 1878, when he resigned. Three years later, he was offered the post of Director of the Conservatoire, which he refused "most emphatically". He considered himself a "poor and inexperienced teacher".

to enumerate all the qualities of your work...." Coming from a leading figure in world music, such praise helped Tchaikovsky to overcome the hurt inflicted by Rubinstein.

The first performance of the concerto was given by Bülow on October 25, 1875, and was hugely successful. At this and Bülow's later performances in the United States, the audience called for the finale to be repeated. The concerto's American reception – and a triumphant first performance in England at London's Crystal Palace in the following March – enabled Tchaikovsky to put up with the criticism (and perhaps envy) of critics at home. The reception given to Tchaikovsky's Piano Concerto No. 1 was an example of the differing responses – critical and popular – to his music.

The concerto contains examples of many of the typical features of Tchaikovsky's music. His liking for drama is seen in the confrontation between the piano and the orchestra. There are two themes – one in the first movement and another in the finale – based on Ukranian folksongs, recalling his love of Kamenka, and another based on a French nursery song which was popular in Russia. His musical ideas are worked out with tremendous force and passion, often conflicting with the musical conventions of the time. These were the elements that appealed to the larger, less aristocratic audiences that were now filling the concert halls of Europe and America, made up of people who wanted to feel emotionally involved in the music they were listening to.

Plans for marriage

But at the moment of his first popular success, a storm was brewing in Tchaikovsky's private life.

The beginnings of the storm are uncertain. But in January 1875, soon after Rubinstein's rejection of the Piano Concerto No. 1, Tchaikovsky wrote to his brother Anatol about his feelings of loneliness. "If it were not for my constant work, I should simply succumb to melancholia," he went on, adding that he felt that he was so undesirable a person that no one wanted to know him. This was by no means the first time that he had, in letters to his family, confessed to feelings of guilt about what he called his "vice" – presumably either homosexual desires or homosexual practices. Almost certainly his sister, Sasha, either by intuition or because he had told her, knew of his sexual inclinations.

He was now in his mid-thirties, with a growing international reputation and approaching his creative peak. The two things missing in his life, gaps from which his fits of depression seemed to spring, were a stable personal relationship and the pleasures of family living. It has been suggested, without any evidence, that his homosexual activities may have led him into danger of blackmail. It is more likely that, at thirty-five, he was hearing the tick of the biological clock. He had realized that if he was to have children he must soon set about it.

The belief was widespread in the nineteenth century that homosexuality was a sickness that could be "cured". Certainly, Tchaikovsky had felt so guilty about his sexuality all his adult life that he would have taken any "cure" available. Whatever the reason, he decided that he must get married.

He announced his decision in a letter to his brother Modest in August 1876. From the start, the plan seemed hardly likely to be successful. "I shall seriously try to enter into legal marriage with someone or other," he wrote. "I am aware that my *inclinations* are the greatest and most unconquerable obstacles to happiness, and I must struggle with my nature with all my strength.... I should like to marry or enter into an open liaison with some woman so as to shut the mouths of contemptible gossipers." Modest and Sasha both tried to deter him. He had no one in particular in mind, and was evidently prepared to marry more to protect his reputation than for any other reason.

Enter Nadia von Meck

At this point, Tchaikovsky's correspondence with Nadia von Meck started. It began quietly enough, with polite exchanges of a commission and of thanks

"Do not worry yourself about my marriage, my angel. The event is not yet imminent, and will certainly not come off before next year. In the course of next month I shall begin to look around and prepare myself a little for matrimony, which for various reasons I consider necessary."
Tchaikovsky, writing to his sister, Sasha, October 1876.

Above: A Moscow concert hall in 1856. It was in a setting like this that many of Tchaikovsky's operas were first performed. Sometimes the tension of a first night was too much for Tchaikovsky to bear, although the audience's reaction mattered less to him than the critics'. Opposite: The same occasion today; the Philharmonic Hall in St. Petersburg.

and, on Nadia's part, admiration for Tchaikovsky's music. But within a few weeks their letters were running to several pages, photographs were exchanged, and they were writing about their most intimate feelings (though not about Tchaikovsky's homosexuality). Anyone reading this correspondence without knowing the facts would suppose that these were love letters. Nadia von Meck generally hid her admiration for the man behind her praise for his music. But as early as March 1877, with the relationship only a few weeks old, she broke out, "Ah God, how great is the man who has power to give others such moments of bliss!" "I venture to believe," Tchaikovsky wrote in reply,

Opposite: A scene from "Swan Lake", written in 1875-6 and Tchaikovsky's first ballet suite. Like many of his other works, it was badly received on its first performance by the Bolshoi Ballet in March 1877. The production was something of a mess. The dancers had complained that part of the score was impossible to dance, so pieces by other composers were substituted. The sets and costumes were from other ballets. The Bolshoi performed "Swan Lake" only a few times and then quietly dropped it. Only after Tchaikovsky's death did it achieve the fame and respect it has today.

"It then became clear that Tchaikovsky had at his first attempt, lifted the whole standard of Russian ballet by creating a masterpiece which has since influenced and inspired many other composers."

Wilson Strutte, on "Swan Lake", from "Tchaikovsky".

"that you have not made a mistake in considering me a kindred spirit."

Early on, Nadia laid down what was to be the main condition of their relationship: they were not to meet. "There was a time when I wished to meet you," she revealed. "Now, the more I am bewitched, the more I fear meeting." Was she merely leading Tchaikovsky on? Would she not have welcomed at least an affair, and possibly marriage, with a man ten years younger whose fame was growing and whose work she so much admired? We shall never know, because at that moment another woman came into Tchaikovsky's life.

Complications

Antonina Milyukova was a twenty-eight-year-old pupil at the Moscow Conservatoire. If she had been in any of Tchaikovsky's classes he had never noticed her. But in May 1877, out of nowhere, she wrote him a letter declaring her love for him.

It was the second letter from an unknown woman that he had received. The letter, and his reply, have both disappeared, but he evidently wrote gently discouraging her. A few days later Antonina wrote again, "After your last letter I loved you twice as much.... There is no fault that could make me stop loving you.... I do not want to look at any other man after you." She immediately followed this up with another letter, fantasizing about killing herself if she could have just one kiss to remember in heaven.

Nineteenth-century letters were often written in flowery and extravagant language. But Antonina Milyukova was "throwing herself" at Tchaikovsky in a way that most people of the time would have thought shameless. She was poor, ill-educated and without the social and cultural background that a famous composer might desire in his wife. Antonina could not have been more different from the woman Tchaikovsky had genuinely loved and wanted to marry – Désirée Artôt, the cultured, cosmopolitan and outstandingly-talented singer.

But it seems that Tchaikovsky accepted that it

was his fate to marry Antonina. After all, hadn't he already, two years before, decided to marry "someone or other"? Here was "someone or other" keen to marry *him!* Perhaps he thought that since she had put herself forward as a potential wife she would do as well as anyone. At any rate, he began to call on her. "It seemed to me now," as he wrote later to Nadia von Meck, "as though some force of fate was driving me to this girl." Within two or three weeks, he had proposed to Antonina.

It was not a romantic proposal. Tchaikovsky told his future bride that although he did not love her he was grateful for her love for him, and they could marry if she wished. Not many women would be happy with such a half-hearted offer, but Antonina accepted it at once.

Normally a man, having become engaged, would take care to spend as much time as possible with his future wife before the wedding, and lose no time in giving the good news to his friends and family. Tchaikovsky did none of these things. Hard at work on his opera *Eugene Onegin,* he went off to the country for a month, leaving Antonina to make the wedding arrangements. Shortly before his return, he announced his forthcoming marriage to his family and to Nadia von Meck. His letter to his brother Anatol was as unenthusiastic as his proposal to Antonina had been. "I am marrying a girl who is not exactly young," he wrote, "but quite passable."

Of his family, Tchaikovsky's eighty-two-year-old father was the only one to show any pleasure. As for Nadia von Meck, she confessed to Tchaikovsky two years later that when she heard the news it was "as though something had snapped in my heart. The thought that you were close to that woman was bitter and unbearable."

The marriage

The marriage took place in Moscow on July 18, 1877. The only witnesses were Tchaikovsky's brother Anatol and his former pupil, Kotek. After the short ceremony, Tchaikovsky and his bride left for

"The moment the wedding was over, and I found myself alone with my wife and realized that our future lot was to be inseparably united, I suddenly realized that I did not feel even ordinarily friendly towards her, but that I abhorred her in the fullest sense. I became certain that I – or, rather, music – the finest and perhaps the only fine part of my being – had died for ever."

Tchaikovsky.

Opposite: The official photograph taken at Tchaikovsky's ill-fated and ill-judged marriage to Antonina Milyukova on July 18, 1877. "I should lie if I said I was happy," Tchaikovsky wrote to his brother two days later. "After such a terrible day as the eighteenth of July, after that ghastly spiritual torture, one cannot recover quickly." In fact, the marriage never recovered. Within three months, it was effectively over.

St. Petersburg to see his father, who was too old and frail to make the journey to Moscow.

The train journey was a nightmare for Tchaikovsky. Alone in the compartment with Antonina, he was brought face to face with what he had done.

She was physically repulsive to him, yet she seemed totally unaware of this. He realized that they had absolutely nothing in common. The fact was that he had married a simple, feather-brained young woman whose interests were completely trivial. He had deluded himself into thinking that at least she admired his music. Now he discovered that she knew nothing of it. It was as if, in their eagerness to get married, they had picked each other's names out of a hat.

Despair

Over the next two weeks, Tchaikovsky's despair deepened. After the visit to his father, the couple visited her people – "a very weird family", according to Tchaikovsky, that argued all the time. He might have hoped, even at this late stage, that Antonina would provide him with the happy family of children he longed for. But it was clear that she had no model of happy family life on which to base one of her own. Any hope that she would be able to provide a social setting in which he could comfortably entertain his friends was soon dashed. In their company she was polite, but clearly overawed and out of her depth with intellectuals.

Soon, Tchaikovsky was making efforts to keep them away from her. By now, he was alternating between bouts of heavy drinking, thoughts of suicide, and writing letters full of self-pity to his family and to Nadia von Meck. At last, pleading the need for isolation to get on with his work, he escaped to Kamenka. "A few more days," he reported to Nadia, "and I swear I should have gone mad."

The story of Tchaikovsky's marriage shows him in his worst light. He must have spent enough time with Antonina before the wedding to know that she would never be able to share his life and interests.

He must also have known what marriage meant physically and that it was doomed.

In the letters written after the wedding, he occasionally mentioned his pity for Antonina, but he showed no real understanding of the distress the marriage must have brought to her too. Many creative people live in a world that seems to revolve entirely around themselves. But Tchaikovsky seemed to be unable to understand that he had brought about his own misery, and his wife's, through sheer foolishness.

He returned from Kamenka to the new apartment that Antonina had been organizing for them in Moscow, ready to start teaching again. His days, spent at the Conservatoire, were now easier, but returning to his wife in the evenings drove him again to despair. One evening he intentionally walked up to his waist in the Moscow River, hoping that this would give him pneumonia or some other fatal illness. In his strange mental state, he had worked out that he could not deliberately commit

The Davidov family. On the left is Lev's sister, Vera, with whom Tchaikovsky had a brief and uncertain love affair in the summer of 1867. Sitting next to her are Sasha and Lev, with their daughter, Anna, on the right. Two more daughters, Tatyana and Natalya, are standing behind, with the three sons, Dmitry, Yury and Vladimir (always known as Bob) in the foreground. In Tchaikovsky's later years, Bob was to become his frequent companion and confidante.

suicide because of the distress this would cause his family, but that there would be nothing wrong in putting himself in death's way. However, he was disappointed. The icy dip did him no harm at all.

The edge of madness

Despite his later claim to have been on the edge of madness, Tchaikovsky was still capable of thinking clearly enough to protect his own interests. He now persuaded his brother Anatol to send him a false telegram saying that he was urgently needed in St. Petersburg on business. There, he had some kind of nervous collapse and was in a coma for two days. He consulted a doctor, who advised that he should never live with, or even see, his wife again. This seems strange advice for a doctor to give, but perhaps Tchaikovsky made it up. Anatol agreed to go to Moscow to explain the situation to Antonina. According to his account he took Nicholas Rubinstein with him, and when they explained the situation Antonina took the news quite calmly, even making a joke about it.

The marriage was at an end, though there was to be no divorce. Antonina had not finished with Tchaikovsky yet, but for the moment his personal crisis seemed to be over. However, with the story of his foolish and failed marriage – and the possible reason for its failure – which was the talk of his friends in Moscow, he felt he must get away. He went to Clarens in Switzerland.

Nadia von Meck's home at Brailov was the focal point of a large estate which her husband had bought. Tchaikovsky stayed as a guest on the estate at the invitation of Nadia von Meck. However, when they both stayed there at the same time, they carefully planned their days so that they would not meet.

Fate

This year, 1877, had seen the importance of Nadia von Meck in his life and the beginning and end of his marriage. But Tchaikovsky had continued to work on his music. At the beginning of the year he had started composing the Fourth Symphony in F Minor, which was to be dedicated to Nadia. In late spring, he had begun an opera based on a narrative poem, *Eugene Onegin,* by the Moscow-born poet, Alexander Pushkin.

By coincidence, *Eugene Onegin* begins with the

heroine, Tatyana, sending a letter to Onegin with whom she has fallen in love. Onegin meets Tatyana and rejects her. Tchaikovsky quickly saw the connection between the events in the story and his own life. His writing of the letter scene in the opera coincided with the arrival of Antonina's first love letters to him, and to judge from what he wrote to Sasha the two became confused in his mind. He confessed to falling in love with Tatyana, the character in the opera. Did he identify Antonina with her? Or did he, perhaps, see the guiding hand of Fate in the coincidence of the fictional and the real letter-writers?

Meanwhile, the Fourth Symphony also reflects the circumstances under which it was written. Tchaikovsky wrote to Nadia von Meck that the symphony's theme was "Fate, the sombre power which prevents the desire for happiness from reaching its goal". Themes in the third and fourth movements suggest ways of escape from Fate's power, such as drinking and dancing, but the symphony ends with the Fate theme triumphant. It is a gloomy work which exactly echoes Tchaikovsky's mood and experiences while he was writing it.

Doomed to isolation

The mental crisis that surrounded Tchaikovsky's marriage was a turning-point in his life. Things were never the same for him again. He was no longer the Conservatoire professor with a life based on Moscow's musical circles. His personal problems had been cruelly exposed to all his friends and had been gossiped about all over the city. His experience had confirmed, as his Fourth Symphony suggested, that Fate could not be ignored or avoided. He felt himself doomed to isolation, peering in through the windows of other people's houses, such as Sasha's, and watching enviously the happy family lives going on inside.

However sympathetic his friends and family felt for him, he had simply walked away from the mess he had made of his life and had left other people to clear it up.

Because of Nadia von Meck's generosity for his financial plight, he managed to obtain a gift of money large enough to clear his debts, and the promise of an annual payment from her.

It was thought necessary to get Antonina out of Moscow, because it was feared that she might do or say something to damage Tchaikovsky's reputation still further. Nicolas Rubinstein and Tchaikovsky's brother Anatol found the money to pack her off to the Black Sea resort of Odessa. From there, Sasha rescued her and took her back to Kamenka. Sasha reported to Tchaikovsky that Antonina wept continually, bit her nails until her hands bled, and had nowhere else to go.

Tchaikovsky showed no sympathy for the wife he had reduced to this state by his desertion. His only reaction was to accuse her, by staying at Kamenka, of keeping him away from his beloved sister and her family.

When Sasha and his brother Modest suggested that, with goodwill on both sides, a reconciliation might be possible, Tchaikovsky rejected the idea angrily. Behind his rage lay the suspicion that Antonina was turning his own family against him.

At last, Antonina left Kamenka, but she continued to write letters to Tchaikovsky – sometimes pleading, sometimes threatening – for the rest of his life. She spent the last twenty-one years of her own life in a mental hospital, where she lived on until 1917.

Wandering in Europe

Meanwhile, with Antonina out of the way, Nadia von Meck's letters reached new depths of intimacy. She assured Tchaikovsky that he had no cause to feel guilty about Antonina, and promised to take care of him financially. Tchaikovsky spent the end of 1877 and the first half of 1878 touring Europe, apparently looking without success for a place to settle. Despite Nadia's assurances, he could not escape from his natural depression, though he managed to complete both the Fourth Symphony and the score of *Eugene Onegin*.

This was the beginning of his return to full-time composition after the stress of his marriage. Although composition took its toll of his health, Tchaikovsky, now thirty-eight, was always at his happiest when writing music. New work flowed from him. He turned now to the sonata form, composing parts for not more than two instruments. In 1878, he wrote his Violin Concerto in D and began a piano sonata. In the same year he began his first orchestral suite and another opera, *The Maid of Orleans*, based on the story of the martyrdom of Joan of Arc. 1880 saw the first performance of the *Italian Capriccio*, and two years later, the Serenade for Strings and the *1812 Overture*.

The *1812* has become one of Tchaikovsky's most popular compositions. It commemorates one of the most famous battles in history – the defeat of Napoleon's army at the gates of Moscow near the end of the Napoleonic wars. Its finale features an exciting contest between sections of the orchestra playing the Russian and French national anthems

The assassination of Tsar Alexander II on March 13, 1881. Tsar for over twenty-five years, Alexander had carried out many great reforms in Russia, including the ending of serfdom. But there was a demand for even greater freedom, and plotters with this aim planted bombs on the Tsar's route to the Winter Palace in St. Petersburg. The second bomb exploded under his carriage, and he died a few hours later.

respectively, and ends with a simulated battle which is often accompanied, in performances today, by cannon and mortar effects.

The piece was commissioned by Nicholas Rubinstein for an industrial exhibition to be held in Moscow in 1881. Tchaikovsky accepted the task reluctantly and dashed the *Overture* off in a week. Although he was prepared to go to great pains over work to which he felt personal commitment, he was also a good "jobbing composer", producing work to order. The occasion of the Moscow Exhibition was to be the Silver Jubilee of Tsar Alexander II, and Tchaikovsky understood exactly what was required of him – a rousing, patriotic piece suitable for a national festival.

He had no illusions about it. "The Overture," he wrote to Nadia von Meck, "will be very noisy. I wrote it without much warmth or enthusiasm. Therefore it has no great artistic value." Tchaikovsky's critics agreed, but not the ordinary music-lovers in his audience. The *1812* has since become one of the standard works in popular concerts of orchestral music all over the world. As it turned out, Tsar Alexander was assassinated in March 1881 and the Exhibition was postponed for a year. The first performance of the *1812 Overture*, when it came, was a reminder of a glorious moment in Russia's history and a suggestion that such heroic times might come again.

The peak of success

Tchaikovsky was now confident of his position in Russian musical and cultural life. He had resigned from the Conservatoire, and in 1881 had turned down the Directorship when it was offered to him on the sudden death of Nicolas Rubinstein. His position in Russian music was safe enough for him to take criticism less to heart. He no longer had to persuade orchestras and soloists to play his work. At the first performance of *The Maid of Orleans* in February 1881 he took no fewer than twenty-four curtain calls. Even the critics were generous with their praise after the first performance in 1882 of the Serenade for Strings.

When he went abroad, he found music-lovers anxious to meet him and praise his work. Thanks to Nadia von Meck, he had no financial worries. He settled into a pleasant annual routine. Usually, in the winter, he would visit western Europe, and later in the year would go to Kamenka or Nadia's estate at Brailov in the Ukraine, where he would compose in peace.

It was at Brailov in 1880 that his relationship with Nadia threatened to take a more serious turn. Despite her professed intention never to meet him, the two had in fact met face to face in Florence in 1878 when she had booked an apartment for him near her own. They had not spoken, but later acknowledged in letters that they had seen each other. This seems a very odd game for grown-up people to play. Maybe Nadia had engineered the whole thing. She may have hoped that something like a romance would develop.

> *"I should like to tell you a great deal about my fantastic feelings towards you, but ... I will only say that this feeling – abstract as it may be – is one of the best and loftiest emotions ever yet experienced by any human being. Therefore you may call me eccentric, or mad, if you please; but you must not laugh at me. All this would be ridiculous, if it were not so sincere and serious."*
>
> Nadia von Meck, writing to Tchaikovsky, February 1877.

Jealousy

In 1880 it seems that Nadia tried to play the same game again. She invited Tchaikovsky to stay at Brailov, and offered him the use of a cottage on the estate. They agreed between themselves the times of their daily walks in the woods so that they would not meet.

But although, according to Tchaikovsky, he kept to the schedule, they one day found themselves approaching each other on the same path. He raised his hat, but did not speak. She seemed confused, and hurried on. The letter she wrote the next day suggested that she had deliberately arranged the meeting and that her feelings for Tchaikovsky were becoming too strong for comfort. "I love to be near you passively, tacitly," she wrote. "To feel you, not as a myth, but as a living man whom I love sincerely." She followed this up with a letter in which she confessed to her jealousy of Antonina at the time of his marriage. "I love you more than anyone and value you above anything else in the world," she went on.

Opposite: After Tchaikovsky's death, the Klin house became a Tchaikovsky Museum, with its rooms left as he had known and lived in them.

Below: The house and garden at Klin, fifty miles from Moscow, where Tchaikovsky settled in 1888. He had first rented a house near Klin three years earlier, but his new home appealed to him because it was more remote from summer visitors and offered the comfort of long walks in the surrounding beechwoods.

Keeping at a distance

Perhaps wiser after his experience with Antonina, Tchaikovsky smelt danger here. Nadia seemed to be moving closer to suggesting marriage, or at least an affair. He certainly did not want this, but he valued their correspondence and wanted to keep their relationship on its former level. Also, if Nadia was really wanting it to become closer, and he rejected her, what would happen to the generous annual allowance she made him? This gave him the financial scurity he needed to compose and freed him from the necessity to teach, which he hated.

For once in his life, Tchaikovsky behaved with care and tact. His music, he told Nadia, was his only true expression of his love for her. In his next few letters, he kept strictly to his music, the work he had in hand, and his methods of composition. Nadia evidently recognized the warning signs, and resumed her former, less intimate tone.

Settling down

In 1884, Tchaikovsky celebrated his forty-fourth birthday. For seven years he had been leading a wandering life, now in Moscow or St. Petersburg, now in France, Italy or Germany, now at Kamenka or Brailov. It was time, he decided, to settle down in a home of his own. In a letter to Nadia he outlined what he had in mind: a modest house standing on its own land, with a garden and some woods nearby where he could walk, a pleasant view, and a reasonable journey time from Moscow.

After some false starts, Tchaikovsky found what he was looking for. It was a house at Maidanovo near Klin, easily reached from Moscow by rail, with a park adjoining the garden and beautiful views. In the spring of 1885, he moved in, and his letters from then on were full of the pleasure of organizing his possessions, taking delivery of his piano, employing servants including an "excellent" cook, and settling in. "What a joy to be in my own home!" he wrote to Nadia. "What a bliss to know that no one will come and interfere with my work, my reading, and my walks!"

A scene from a modern Russian production of "Vakula the Smith". This was composed for a competition but Tchaikovsky failed to realize the closure date was a year away. It still won the prize, but flopped when it was first performed two years later. In 1885, Tchaikovsky reworked it and renamed it "Cherevichki". This time, it was a success.

Although he was to move to other houses before settling finally in 1892, his home was to be in or near Klin for the rest of his life. In his own solitary way he was able to capture some of the peace that he had experienced for so long on his visits to Kamenka.

Slaying a dragon

No one laughed at Tchaikovsky any more. In 1885 he was elected Director of the Moscow branch of the Russian Musical Society, which had given him his first job as a young teacher. About the same time he began work on a symphony based on *Manfred,* a poem by the English poet Byron, a project that had been around for some years, and a new opera, *The Sorceress.*

In the same year, there was a sign of Tchaikovsky's growing confidence in his own work. He had always hated looking back over his earlier compositions, but in 1885 he took out the score of an early opera, which had failed eleven years before, *Vakula the Smith.* Tchaikovsky rewrote his original version so much that he gave it the new title of *Cherevichki.*

He conducted the first three performances of *Cherevichki,* in January 1887, himself. This was also a sign of his growing confidence. Nearly twenty years earlier, his first experience of conducting had been a disaster. Paralyzed with nervousness, he had reached the conductor's desk unable to remember the music or read the score. He had fumbled his way through, giving the leads to the orchestra at the wrong moment or to the wrong instruments, forcing the musicians to ignore him. Fortunately, the orchestra knew the music – a selection of dances from his opera *The Voyevoda* – so well that they put up a good performance. It was not surprising that Tchaikovsky did not want to go through an experience like that again.

But despite nervous qualms and a sick headache before the first night of *Cherevichki,* he conducted well and received a huge ovation. "Everyone praised me," he reported. "They said they had no idea I possessed such a gift for conducting."

A few weeks later he conducted a concert in St. Petersburg. His new career as a conductor had begun. It was to take him all over Europe and to the United States, and make him an international musical star. After twenty years, he had slain one of his dragons.

Furious activity

But only one. Tchaikovsky's doubts about his musical ability and his personal worth were so strong that no amount of reassurance, no standing ovations, no critical praise could banish them. He was also – in his late forties – increasingly aware of the passing of time. "If only I were twenty years younger!" he exlaimed in a letter to Nadia. "How short life is!" he wrote in his diary. "How much I still have to do, to think and to say! We keep putting things off and meanwhile death lurks round the corner."

Perhaps it was this thought that tempted Tchaikovsky into a phase of furious activity. In 1888 and again in 1889 he made concert tours in Europe. He was now a member not merely of the Russian, but of the world musical establishment. On his visits abroad, he rubbed shoulders with its older generation such as Brahms and with relative newcomers like Grieg and the thirty-year-old British composer Ethel Smyth. But self-doubt would not go away. "Every hour I ask myself – why?" he wrote after giving a concert in London in 1889. "Is it worthwhile? And I come to the conclusion that it is far better to live quietly, without fame."

Between the concert tours he was composing relentlessly. The year 1888 saw the completion of his Fifth Symphony in E Minor and the fantasy overture to *Hamlet*. The following year, he wrote his ballet music for *The Sleeping Beauty* as well as several minor pieces. An opera, *The Queen of Spades*, followed in 1890, together with a string sextet, *Souvenir de Florence*. But the major event of 1890 in Tchaikovsky's life, not directly connected with his music, was a shattering one.

"Something very important happened today. I conducted the first orchestral rehearsal in such style that all were astonished (unless it were mere flattery), for they had expected I should make a fool of myself.... Now I know I can conduct, I shall not be nervous at the performance."

Tchaikovsky, writing to his brother, Modest, December 1886.

A break with the past

There had been nothing to suggest that the letter that arrived on October 4, 1890 from Nadia von Meck would not be simply the latest instalment of the correspondence – delightful to both parties – which had now been going on for fourteen years. In fact, it was a bombshell. Nadia wrote that she was on the edge of bankruptcy. The annual allowance she had been paying the fifty-year-old Tchaikovsky must end. She added that their friendship must also end. "Do not forget me, and think of me sometimes," she concluded.

Tchaikovsky's reaction was many-sided. He was no longer the poor composer, living from hand to mouth, that he had been in 1876. He did not need Nadia's money. In fact his brother-in-law, Leo Davidov, had often advised him to end the arrangement. But he resented Nadia's suggestion that *because* she could no longer pay him their friendship was over.

In his reply, he protested: "Do you really think me incapable of remembering you when I no longer receive your money? How could I forget for a moment all you have done for me, and all for which I owe you gratitude?... I kiss your hands, with all my heart's warmth, and implore you to believe, once and for all, that no one feels more keenly for your troubles than I do." He ended with a promise to write again "about myself and all I am doing" – a clear sign that he could not believe that the correspondence had ended.

There was no reply. Tchaikovsky wrote again several times, with the same result. Then he tried writing to Nadia's son-in-law, who replied that she was too ill to write and returned his letter. The composer and his patron never corresponded again. The strange friendship was over.

Opposite: Tchaikovsky in 1889. By now he was internationally-successful both as composer and conductor. It was in this year that he finished the second of his three enduring suites of ballet music, "The Sleeping Beauty". It was first performed in St. Petersburg in January 1890 at a gala première in the presence of Tsar Alexander III. The Tsar's only comment was, "Very nice." Again, the public failed to respond to Tchaikovsky's work, and "The Sleeping Beauty" achieved popularity only after the composer's death.

Panic

No doubt Tchaikovsky was deeply hurt by the sudden and unexplained end of a friendship that had lasted for fourteen years – more than a quarter of his life. But his immediate reaction was one of panic over money. "Now I must start quite a fresh life, on a totally different scale of expenditure," he wrote to his friend and publisher Peter Jurgenson. "In all probability I shall be compelled to seek some occupation in St. Petersburg which will bring me in a good salary. This is very, very humiliating – yes, humiliating is the word." This was an exaggeration, illustrating Tchaikovsky's lifelong readiness to believe that disaster was only just round the corner.

In reality, it was his pride that was hurt, and the pain increased when he discovered that Nadia was not really in financial difficulties. She had merely used this excuse to end their friendship. "I could not conceive change in anyone so half-divine," Tchaikovsky wrote to her son-in-law. "Never in my life have I felt so lowered, or my pride so profoundly injured as in this matter." The shock remained with him for the rest of his life. He often spoke of Nadia with love and regret, and sometimes with bitterness. Hers was the last name he spoke before he died.

Why did Nadia act so strangely? There is no easy explanation. She seems to have been suffering from some kind of nervous illness, but in such circumstances most people would draw their old friends closer rather than reject them. The answer may be that just as she began her correspondence with Tchaikovsky on a casual whim, she ended it in the same way.

America

In 1889 a young conductor and impresario, Walter Damrosch, persuaded an American millionaire, Andrew Carnegie, to finance the building of a new concert hall for New York. The original name was the Music Hall, but it later became Carnegie Hall. The opening season was planned for 1891, and Walter Damrosch set about organizing a great opening festival. He was an admirer of Tchaikovsky's music, and planned that the main piece of the festival should be a concert in which Tchaikovsky would conduct some of his own works. This would be a great feather in Damrosch's cap, and good publicity for the opening of the new hall.

"I am convinced that I am ten times more famous in America than in Europe.... Several of my works, which are unknown even in Moscow, are frequently played here. I am a much more important person here than in Russia. Is that not curious?"

Tchaikovsky, during his tour of America, April 1891.

By 1891, when Tchaikovsky visited the United States, New York had become America's leading commercial city. Its old markets and slum areas stood cheek-by-jowl with the first skyscrapers. The bustling life of the streets, which Tchaikovsky observed as he made his way to his hotel, contrasted sharply with the fine dresses and delicate manners of New York's "high society" who came to his concerts. He conducted four concerts in New York before moving on to Baltimore and Philadelphia, taking in visits to Washington and the Niagara Falls.

The invitation to Tchaikovsky arrived when he was still smarting from Nadia's break with him, and he eagerly accepted it. In March 1891 he set out from home, going via Berlin and Paris before boarding the liner *Le Bretagne* at Le Havre.

He began his journey in a cheerful mood, but his natural gloom and foreboding soon set in. By the time he reached France he was dreading the voyage and the reception that awaited him in America. "In these last three days," he wrote to a friend, "I have become simply sick from despair, fear, and the worst depression." He had hoped, on his journey, to work on the *Nutcracker* ballet music which had been commissioned by the St. Petersburg opera, but his mood made this impossible.

51

There was worse to come. In Paris, on April 15, he casually picked up a Russian newspaper and read the news that his beloved sister Sasha had died a week before. She was forty-eight, and had been ill for some time. Because of her illness, and because Tchaikovsky now had a country home of his own, his summer visits to Kamenka had been less frequent in recent years, but she had been one of the few firm anchors in his life. As his brother Modest wrote, "She, who had been to him a haven and a refuge from all the troubles of life ... for, together with Nadia von Meck, she had been his chief support, making him welcome, and bestowing upon him the most affectionate attention."

Any hope Tchaikovsky might have had of working on the voyage was dispelled by the gale-tossed crossing and by the urgings of the other first class passengers, once they discovered who he was, to play for them. On arrival in New York, characteristically Tchaikovsky wrote in his diary that "in my heart there were a despair and a desire to run miles and miles away." But there were too many visitors to be received, visits to be made and rehearsals to be attended for even a born depressive to spare much time for his own thoughts and feelings.

More success

The inaugural concert at Carnegie Hall was on May 5, 1891. Tchaikovsky conducted his *Coronation March*, composed in 1883. It was "loudly received", he wrote in his diary.

The wildest praise of New York's music critics was reserved for the third of the Carnegie Hall concerts. Tchaikovsky conducted his Suite No. 3 in G, written in 1884. This, wrote the *New York World*, "has the magnitude of a symphony. It is made up of a series of four numbers and lasts altogether nearly an hour. Each number is of rare interest and strange musical beauty." The *Evening Post* described the suite as "one of [Tchaikovsky's] most inspired and characteristic works." The *Morning Journal* called the suite "a train of beautiful thoughts, like a gorgeous pageant." The *Brooklyn*

Daily Eagle found it "a fresh, fascinating work, filled with the modern spirit yet rich in melody."

Even Tchaikovsky could not fail to be pleased by such unanimous praise, though he wondered to his diary whether "the Americans overdo it too much". But the attention was welcome. "The press sings hallelujahs to me that I could never dream to hear in Russia," he wrote to Modest.

The "Nutcracker"

Soon after his return to Russia, Tchaikovsky summed up his feelings about his visit to his publisher, Peter Jurgenson. "In general I am very satisfied with my trip to America," he revealed. "I enjoy remembering how enthusiastically they received me, how obliging, affectionate, friendly everyone was to me... I left having promised to come to America again and even gave them the hope of my coming in January of next winter." But his immediate task was to get down to the *Nutcracker* ballet music. He had already postponed once the deadline for its completion.

In the end, negotiations for a second visit to the United States broke down over the question of fees. But his single visit ensured the continuing popularity of his music in America. It also paved the way for a succession of European composers who were to cross the Atlantic, and played an important part in broadening American musical interest in Europe.

The *Nutcracker* was given its first performance at St. Petersburg in December 1892, but aroused little interest. None of Tchaikovsky's ballet music, such as *Swan Lake* (1875-6), *The Sleeping Beauty* (1889) and the *Nutcracker,* was much appreciated during the composer's lifetime. This is surprising, because most people today would agree with the writer Humphrey Searle when he described Tchaikovsky as "the ballet composer *par excellence*".

There were two possible reasons for his late recognition as a composer for the ballet. One is that his music was thought too difficult to dance to; part of the *Nutcracker* was dropped from the first performance for this reason. The other may

The 1988 production of Tchaikovsky's "Casse-Noisette" (The Nutcracker). This was Tchaikovsky's last ballet suite, composed between February 1891 and April 1892. On this occasion, even Tsar Alexander III was full of compliments, but yet again the production was reviled by the critics. Tchaikovsky himself admitted that he found it "a little boring, despite the magnificence of the setting". Later ballet lovers did not agree.

be that his music was too *musical*. In nineteenth-century Russian ballet, the music was regarded merely as an accompaniment to the dance. It was not required, or even expected, to have any merit of its own.

Ballet was very much the "poor relation" of opera and – until very late in the nineteenth century – did not attract the talent and public interest that it now has. What happened to Tchaikovsky's original *Swan Lake* was typical. It was first performed with second-hand costumes on a set made up of scenery left over from an opera production. Whole sections of Tchaikovsky's music were cut out because they were too "difficult", and other pieces by other composers dropped in. By the end of all this, nearly a third of the music used in the original 1877 performance was not Tchaikovsky's.

It was in 1894 that the Russian choreographer

Marius Petipa went back to Tchaikovsky's original score and looked at it again. He choreographed a whole new production from it, first performed in 1895, and this was the start of *Swan Lake's* new life as one of the great romantic ballets as they are performed today all over the world. It was also the start of Tchaikovsky's recognition as a masterly composer for the ballet. After seeing the 1921 production of *The Sleeping Beauty,* the composer Stravinsky wrote to the producer, Sergei Diaghilev, that "Tchaikovsky's outstanding gift for melody explains a great deal of his success as a ballet composer. For it is melody and rhythm which are essential to all ballet music." In fact, many Tchaikovsky pieces not originally written for the ballet, such as his *Romeo and Juliet* overture and even parts of his Fifth Symphony, have been used as the basis of ballet productions with huge success.

Another move

In the summer of 1892, Tchaikovsky moved to another house at Klin which was to be his last home. There, he started work on a new symphony, in E flat. This was the only one of his major projects that he abandoned, though he used part of it for the first movement of his Piano Concerto No. 3. The next year, he began what most critics agree is his finest work, the Sixth Symphony in B Minor. He worked steadily at it through the early months of 1893, though he was interrupted by a previous engagement to conduct a concert in London and then travel to Cambridge to receive the honorary degree of Doctor of Music. By late July, he was back and a few days later he wrote to his nephew, Vladimir Davidov, that the symphony was "quite the best – and especially the most 'sincere' – of all my works. I love it as I never loved any one of my musical offerings before."

The Sixth Symphony was given its first performance in St. Petersburg on October 28, 1893, with Tchaikovsky conducting. It was at the last minute that he gave it its title *Pathetique*. The suggestion was his brother Modest's. As happened so often in Tchaikovsky's life, response to the first performance was muted. It was only after his death that it was seen as the most powerful and majestic of his music.

Subsequent events, and the romantic inventions of some writers, have made it difficult to assess the symphony on its musical merit alone. Some writers have said that it is a sound-picture of Tchaikovsky's life. Others have called it a reflection on the inevitable pattern of life as he saw it – hope, love, disappointment, and finally failure. It has even been called the "Suicide" Symphony. One well-respected critic, James Gibbons Huneker, wrote of the finale of the Sixth Symphony that "the atmosphere of grief, immutable, eternal, hovers about like a huge black-winged angel."

On October 31, 1893, Tchaikovsky went to a play in St. Petersburg. On November 1, he joined friends for supper at a restaurant. The next morning, he did not come down to breakfast, complaining of

"O God, how short life is! How much I have yet to accomplish before it is time to leave off! How many projects! When I am quite well – as I am at present – I am seized with a feverish thirst for work, but the thought of the shortness of human life paralyses all my energy."

Tchaikovsky, writing to
Nadia von Meck, August 1886.

indigestion and a bad night's sleep. This was nothing new. He had had vague digestive problems for years and was also prone to bouts of sleeplessness. Later that morning, he went out to visit a friend but soon returned, still feeling unwell. He joined Modest and Vladimir Davidov for lunch, but ate nothing. As they sat talking, he poured himself a glass of water and drank it.

Within hours, he was feeling worse. A doctor was called and diagnosed cholera – the almost inevitably fatal disease that had carried off Tchaikovsky's mother. The guess was that the water Tchaikovsky had drunk at the lunch table had been unboiled and contained cholera germs. According to Modest's account, Tchaikovsky's illness seems to have followed the classic pattern of cholera: first, nausea and vomiting, then kidney failure and delirium, and finally fever. Death came early in the morning of November 6, 1893. Tchaikovsky was fifty-three years old.

The Tchaikovsky Memorial outside the Moscow Conservatoire.

Questions

Questions about the manner of Tchaikovsky's death began almost at once. Why had he been so foolhardy as to drink unboiled water in a city where he knew a cholera epidemic was raging? Why had the others round the table not stopped him? Could his death in fact have been suicide? Could he have slipped poison into his drink of water at the table? People remembered that he had attempted suicide in the river many years before.

It was noted, too, that the only account of Tchaikovsky's death came from Modest, who had long ago appointed himself the guardian of his brother's reputation and perhaps could not be trusted to tell the truth.

Then there was the Sixth Symphony. This, soon after it was performed at a memorial concert for the composer shortly after his death, came to be seen as his own obituary, perhaps even as his suicide note. But no one had suspected this on its first performance. Indeed, no one thought much of the symphony at all.

Above: Tchaikovsky's name is perpetuated in the International Tchaikovsky Contests held in the Moscow Conservatoire.
Right: The Russian pianist, Ivo Pogovelich, for whom Tchaikovsky's nationalistic music must be especially meaningful.

In 1981, a story surfaced from a Russian who had emigrated to the West which seemed to back the poison theory. It was that Tchaikovsky had been threatened with the exposure of his homosexual activities and was offered the alternative of poisoning himself. The story sounds very dark and dramatic, and was later backed by a second source, but it still seems unlikely, raising more questions than it answers. It may have been merely second- or third-hand gossip.

The truth of the matter will probably never be known now. But in many people's minds the story persists that the theme of the Sixth Symphony is a losing struggle with fate and that, when he was writing it, Tchaikovsky knew that the end was near.

Tchaikovsky's combination of melody, emotion and often melancholy exerts a powerful appeal which was largely lost on the audiences and critics of his own time. Today, however, Tchaikovsky is one of the more accessible composers. These young musicians in a detention camp for Vietnamese refugees in Hong Kong show the intensity of their response.

Music for the world

Tchaikovsky was the first composer to achieve a world-wide reputation in his own lifetime. He was the first to unlock Russian music for the rest of the world to appreciate. He also freed concert music from the restricting influence of the Conservatoires and made it available to large numbers of ordinary people. In this he was helped by the increasing fashion in the late nineteenth century for huge concert halls seating thousands. In some of the orchestral effects he tried to achieve, and in his ballet music, he was ahead of his time, so that they came to be appreciated only after his death.

Popularity

He influenced not only the Russian composers who followed him but also composers such as Sibelius and Dvŏrák. The Russian composer Prokofiev, the first serious composer to write music for films, copied many of the dramatic effects that Tchaikovsky liked to create. It is no accident that Tchaikovsky's own music has been used in many movies.

After his death, the house at Klin became the Tchaikovsky Museum. When the Russian Revolution came in 1917, Tchaikovsky's music was dismissed as decadent and irrelevant to the revolutionary struggle, but the Museum was kept open and survived until Tchaikovsky was "approved" once again. It was badly damaged during the German occupation of Russia during World War II, but was later restored. Near the end of World War II, when Soviet forces joined in the defeat of Germany, there was a new wave of enthusiasm in Britain and America for all things Russian. Tchaikovsky's music reached new heights of popularity which it has maintained ever since. His First, Fourth and Sixth Symphonies and his piano concertos, in particular, are played frequently by most of the world's leading orchestras. *Swan Lake*, the *Nutcracker* and the *Sleeping Beauty* are in the repertoires of the major international ballet companies. Movements from these and other works, such as the waltz from his opera *Eugene Onegin,* are often played in concerts of light music.

Tchaikovsky's life was one of despair and gloom lightened by only brief moments of happiness. Yet he left behind music which has given deep pleasure to millions of people all over the world, and which opened the world's ears to Russia's musical riches.

"The real tragedy of Tchaikovsky is that he spent a great part of his life under the shadow of imaginary horrors created by his own sensitive and tortured nature. And just as he was emerging from this shadow, just as he was achieving an emotional balance and maturity, just as he was reaching the height of his creative powers, the imaginary horrors became a reality and Fate, that great Russian obsession, struck him down."

Wilson Strutte,
from "Tchaikovsky".

Musical terms

Arrangement: The adaptation of a piece of music for instruments other than those for which it was originally written.

Ballet: A dramatic form of dancing that uses set steps and techniques and is usually performed with a musical accompaniment.

Chord: The term used to describe three or more notes sounded simultaneously.

Concerto: A musical work, usually in three *movements*, for orchestra and one or more *solo* instruments.

Duet: A piece of music written for two performers.

Harmony: The combination of musical notes, sounded simultaneously, to form *chords*.

Movement: A self-contained section of a large composition. Each section has its own key, tempo and structure. A large composition that does not have any such sections is described as being "in one movement".

Opera: A dramatic work in which all or most of the performers sing their parts. Opera, as it is known today, was first performed in Italy in the early 1600s.

Overture: A piece of orchestral music that introduces an *opera*, *ballet* or other large work. An overture is often performed as a piece on its own.

Quartet: A piece of music written for four performers.

Sextet: A piece of music written for six performers.

Solo: A piece of music written for one performer.

Sonata: A composition that is made up of several *movements*, for a *solo* instrument, or *solo* instrument and piano.

Suite: Originally, a collection of musical pieces, usually dances, that were to be played in succession. Today, the term is used to describe a set of *movements* from an *opera* or *ballet* that are to be played as one instrumental piece.

Symphony: A long composition for orchestra. It is usually in the form of a *sonata* and made up of three or four *movements*.

Variations: Modifications made to a passage of music, so that the original passage is still recognizable. The variation can be of *harmony*, melody, rhythm, tonality or texture.

Important Dates

1840   May 7: Peter Ilyich Tchaikovsky is born in Votinsk, Russia.

1848   The Tchaikovsky family moves to Moscow and then to St. Petersburg.

1850   Tchaikovsky starts at the School of Jurisprudence in St. Petersburg to be trained as a government servant.

1854   Tchaikovsky's mother dies of cholera. Tchaikovsky begins to take an interest in music. He starts piano and singing lessons.

1859   Tchaikovsky, aged nineteen, becomes a clerk in the Ministry of Justice in St. Petersburg.

1861   July: Tchaikovsky visits Germany, Belgium, France and Britain. He returns to St. Petersburg three months later.

1862   Tchaikovsky begins studying at the St. Petersburg Conservatoire, while still working at the Ministry of Justice.

1863   Tchaikovsky, aged twenty-three, resigns from his job and begins full-time study at the Conservatoire.

1865   Tchaikovsky graduates from the St. Petersburg Conservatoire with a diploma.

1866   Jan: Tchaikovsky becomes a tutor in harmony at the Moscow Conservatoire. While composing his First Symphony, he has a nervous breakdown. He is ordered to take a complete rest from playing and composing.

1868   Feb: Tchaikovsky's First Symphony is performed in its entirety. Tchaikovsky, aged twenty-nine, becomes engaged to a Belgian opera singer, Désirée Artôt.

1869   After learning that Désirée Artôt has married a Spanish singer in Warsaw, Tchaikovsky begins a period of intense composition.

1872   Tchaikovsky composes his Second Symphony.

1874   Tchaikovsky's first opera, *Vakula the Smith*, wins a prize competition, but is a failure in performance. He begins writing his Piano Concerto No. 1.

1875   Tchaikovsky composes his Third Symphony.
        The Moscow Opera commissions the ballet music, *Swan Lake*.
        Oct 25: The first performance of Piano Concerto No. 1 is given in the United States. It is a huge success.

1876   Tchaikovsky's correspondence begins with Nadia von Meck.

1877   July 18: Peter Ilyich Tchaikovsky marries Antonina Milyukova. He realizes it is a mistake and goes into deep despair.
        Oct: Tchaikovsky's doctor orders him not to see Antonina again: the marriage is over.
        Nadia von Meck promises to give Tchaikovsky an annual allowance.
        Tchaikovsky starts a tour of Europe.

1878   Returning to Moscow, Tchaikovsky finishes his Fourth Symphony and begins a period of full-time composition. He writes a violin concerto and begins a piano sonata, his First Orchestral Suite and an opera, *The Maid of Orleans*. Tchaikovsky resigns as tutor from the Moscow Conservatoire.

1880   Tchaikovsky begins his Piano Concerto No. 2 and writes the *1812* Overture. His father dies.

1881   Feb: *The Maid of Orleans* is performed for the first time and is widely acclaimed.
        Tchaikovsky declines the post of Director of the Moscow Conservatoire.

1885   Tchaikovsky sets up his own country home near Klin. He writes the *Manfred* Symphony and a new opera, *The Sorceress*.
        He is elected Director of the Moscow branch of the Russian Musical Society.

1887   Jan: Tchaikovsky conducts the first three performances of *Cherevichki*, a revised version of his first opera, *Vakula the Smith*.

1888   Tchaikovsky undertakes his first international tour as a conductor.

1889   Tchaikovsky finishes the ballet music for *The Sleeping Beauty*.

1890   Tchaikovsky writes another opera, *The Queen of Spades*.
        After fourteen years, Tchaikovsky's correspondence with Nadia von Meck ends abruptly.

1891   Mar: Tchaikovsky travels to the United States to take part in the opening festival of the Carnegie Hall in New York, which is to be held in May. He goes on to conduct concerts in Baltimore and Philadelphia.

1892   Mar: The *Nutcracker* is performed for the first time. Tchaikovsky starts work on his Sixth Symphony.

1893   Tchaikovsky travels to Britain to receive the honorary degree of Doctor of Music at Cambridge University.
On his return, he completes the Sixth Symphony, known as the *Pathétique*.
Oct 28: The first performance of the Sixth Symphony is given in St. Petersburg.
Nov 2: Tchaikovsky contracts cholera.
Nov 6: Peter Ilyich Tchaikovsky, aged fifty-three, dies in St. Petersburg.

Recommended Listening:

1st String Quartet: Listen especially to the slow movement. This features a Russian folk song which the composer heard a carpenter sing outside his room.

The Nutcracker Suite: This is a collection of dances from Tchaikovsky's ballet which describes a Christmas when a little girl's presents come to life. The suite includes the famous Dance of the Sugar Plum Fairy which features a new instrument – the Celesta – a small piano in which the hammers hit tiny metal bars producing a silvery bell-like sound.

1st Piano Concerto: Tchaikovsky dedicated this to Nicolas Rubinstein – Director of the Moscow Conservatoire. When Rubinstein played it for the first time, he disliked it so much that he threw the music onto the floor! This has become one of Tchaikovsky's best-known works.

Violin Concerto: This beautiful work was first performed in New York.

Italian Capriccio: One of Tchaikovsky's happiest works.

Sixteen Songs for Children: These short songs are based on Russian melodies.

Romeo and Juliet – Fantasy Overture: Tchaikovsky chooses events from Shakespeare's famous love story and paints a musical picture. The well-known "Love" theme is played on muted violas and cor anglais. The "Fight" theme features cymbal crashes to represent the clash of swords, and the end of the tragedy is heralded by muffled drum beats.

1812 Overture: This was written for full orchestra *plus* military band, bells and cannon! This music, which depicts the battle between Napoleon and the Russians, features a Russian hymn, and the French National anthem. The bells peal out in triumph at the end.

Index

α

LAKE COUNTY PUBLIC LIBRARY
INDIANA

THIS BOOK IS RENEWABLE BY PHONE OR IN PERSON IF THERE IS NO RESERVE
WAITING OR FINE DUE.   LCP #0390